TICK TOCK
BUZZ
6:00
CUCKO
ZZ

If you were

Onomatopoeia

onomatopoeia (on-oh-ma-toe-pee-ah)
a word that sounds like the action it describes

SNAP!
STOMP! STOMP!
Pat! Pat!
CLAP! CLAP!

by Trisha Speed Shaskan   illustrated by Sara Gray

PICTURE WINDOW BOOKS
Minneapolis, Minnesota

Editor: Christianne Jones
Designer: Tracy Davies
Page Production: Melissa Kes
Art Director: Nathan Gassman
The illustrations in this book were created with acrylics.

Picture Window Books
5115 Excelsior Boulevard
Suite 232
Minneapolis, MN 55416
877-845-8392
www.picturewindowbooks.com

Library of Congress Cataloging-in-Publication Data
Shaskan, Trisha Speed, 1973-
If you were onomatopoeia / by Trisha Speed
Shaskan ; illlustrated by Sara Gray.
p. cm. — (Word fun)
Includes index.
ISBN 978-1-4048-4098-0 (lib. bdg.)
1. English language—Onomatopoeic words—Juvenile
literature. 2. Sounds, Words for—Juvenile literature.
I. Gray, Sara, ill. II. Title.
PE1597.S53 2008
428.1—dc22
                                    2007044144

Looking for onomatopoeia?

Watch for the big, colorful words in the example sentences.

Special thanks to our advisers for their expertise:

Rosemary G. Palmer, Ph.D., Department of Literacy
College of Education, Boise State University

Susan Kesselring, M.A., Literacy Educator
Rosemount—Apple Valley—Eagan (Minnesota) School District

If you were onomatopoeia ...

3

... you could CHOO! CHOO! or WOO! WOO! like a train.

CHOO CHOO

WOO WOO

You could **DRIP, DROP, DRIP, DROP** like a leaky faucet.

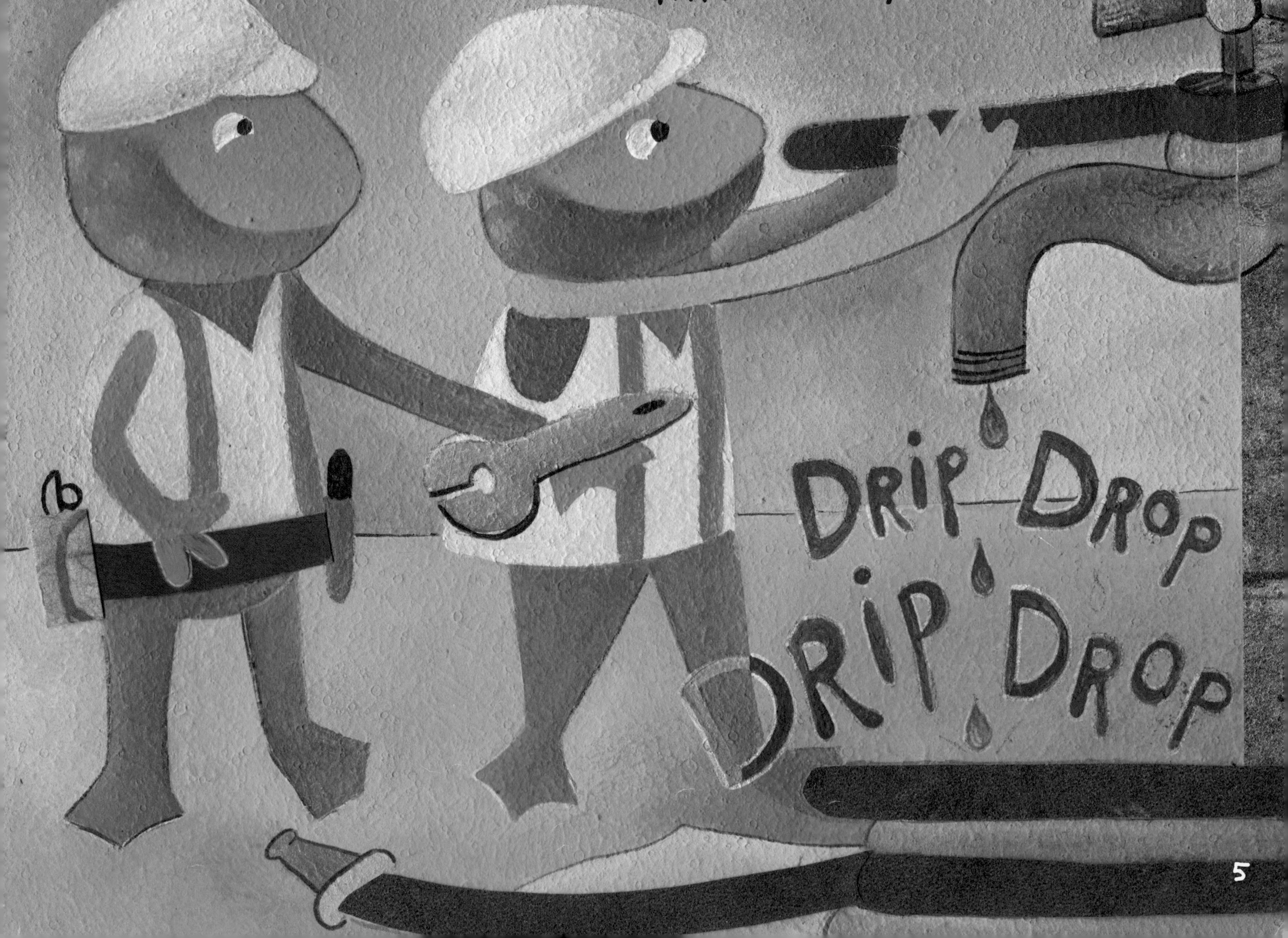

If you were onomatopoeia, you would be a word that sounds like the action it describes. It would be your job to imitate the sounds that surround you.

You could **KER-PLUNK** and **SPLASH** like a fish jumping into water.

If you were onomatopoeia, you would need to be an attentive listener. Being attentive means to listen carefully and concentrate on what you hear. You could imitate the sounds you hear indoors.

POP

CLANG

You could **CLANG** like a pot or **POP** like corn.

You could **WHiR** like a blender.

9

If you were onomatopoeia, you could sound like nature.

You could WHOOSH like a waterfall,

WHISPER like the wind,

SWIRL and TWIRL like a tornado,

SPLISH and **SPLOSH**
like the rain,

or **BooM** like thunder.

If you were onomatopoeia, you could make animal sounds.
Animals use sounds to communicate.

ROAR

GRRR!

GRRR!

You could **ROAR** like a lion that
rounds up its cubs. **GRRR! GRRR!**

f you were onomatopoeia, you could explore how one
nimal sound can be heard in a variety of ways
ecause different languages are made
p of different sounds.

You could bark like a
dog in English: WOOF!
WOOF!

WOOF! WOOF!

You could call out "**JUG-O-RUM**" like a bullfr
does when it marks its home turf.

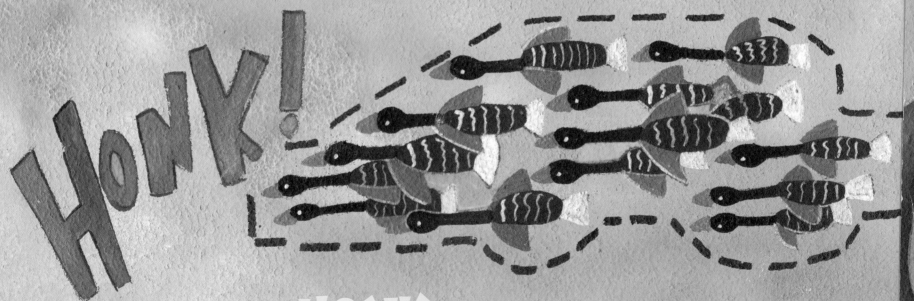

You could **HONK** like a gaggle of geese
when they fly through the air.

If you were onomatopoeia, you could name the sounds you can make with your hands or feet.

You could say "STOMP! STOMP!" and "SNAP! SNAP!"

If you were onomatopoeia, you could create music by making percussion sounds. Percussion instruments create sound when they are struck or shook.

You could make the
TSST-TUT-TAH, TSST-TUT-TAH
sound like a brush on a cymbal.

You could BANG! BANG! BANG! and
RAT-A-TAT-TAT like a stick on a drum.

If you were onomatopoeia, you could make the sounds that keep time.

You could **TICK** and **TOCK** like a clock, or **BUZZ** like an alarm.

TICK

TOCK

ZZZUB

6:00

You could **CUCKOO** like the bird that marks each hour.

When the sun comes up, you could COCK-A-DOODLE-DOO, and when the moon rises you could AH-OOOOO ...

Cock-a-doodle-doo

... if you were onomatopoeia.

ah-ooooo

22

FUN WITH ONOMATOPOEIA

Pack a notebook and a pencil and go outside with a friend.

Go to a park, or just step outside into your own back yard.

Listen to the sounds that surround you. You may hear the sounds of cars passing by or dogs barking. Write down the sounds you hear and label them. For example, a dog barking: Woof! Woof! Record at least 10 sounds. Try to listen carefully for sounds you don't usually hear, like footsteps on the ground. Compare your list of sounds to a friend's. Did you hear the same things?

Glossary

attentive—to listen carefully and concentrate on what you hear

communicate—to exchange information

imitate—to copy

onomatopoeia—a word that sounds like the action it describes

percussion—instruments that create sound when they are struck or shook

To Learn More

More Books to Read

Johnson, David A. *Snow Sounds: An Onomatopoeic Story.* New York: Houghton Mifflin, 2006.

Murphy, Yannick. *Ahwooooooooo!* New York: Clarion, 2006.

Park, Linda Sue, and Julia Durango. *Yum! Yuck! A Foldout Book of People Sounds.* Watertown, Mass.: Charlesbridge, 2005.

On the Web

FactHound offers a safe, fun way to find Web sites related to topics in this book. All of the sites on FactHound have been researched by our staff.

1. Visit *www.facthound.com*
2. Type in this special code: 1404840982
3. Click on the FETCH IT button.

Your trusty FactHound will fetch the best sites for you!

24

Index

onomatopoeia as
animal sounds, 12–13, 22
different languages, 14–15
hands and feet sounds, 16–17
indoor sounds, 8–9
nature sounds, 10–11
percussion sounds, 18–19
time sounds, 20–21

Look for all of the books in the Word Fun series:

If You Were a Conjunction
If You Were a Homonym or a Homophone
If You Were a Noun
If You Were a Palindrome
If You Were a Preposition
If You Were a Pronoun
If You Were a Synonym
If You Were a Verb
If You Were Alliteration
If You Were an Adjective
If You Were an Adverb
If You Were an Antonym
If You Were an Interjection
If You Were Onomatopoeia